WITHDRAWN

# HIDING IN THE
# POLAR REGIONS

## Deborah Underwood

Heinemann Library
Chicago, Illinois

## www.heinemannraintree.com
Visit our website to find out more information about Heinemann-Raintree books.

## To order:
☎ Phone 888-454-2279
💻 Visit www.heinemannraintree.com to browse our catalog and order online.

Edited by Rebecca Rissman and Nancy Dickmann
Designed by Joanna Hinton Malivoire
Picture research by Tracy Cummins
Originated by Capstone Global Library
Printed and bound in China by Leo Paper Products Ltd

15 14 13 12 11
10 9 8 7 6 5 4 3 2 1

**Library of Congress Cataloging-in-Publication Data**
Underwood, Deborah.
  Hiding in the polar regions / Deborah Underwood.
-- 1st ed. p. cm. -- (Creature camouflage)
  Includes bibliographical references and index.
  ISBN 978-1-4329-4027-0 (hc) -- ISBN 978-1-4329-4036-2 (pb) 1.  Animals--Polar regions--Juvenile literature. 2. Camouflage (Biology)--Juvenile literature.  I. Title.
  QL104.U53 2010
  591.47'2--dc22
                    2009051778

**Acknowledgments**
The author and publisher are grateful to the following for permission to reproduce copyright material: pp. FLPA 6 (Hannu Hautala), 7 (Imagebroker/Jonathan Carlile) 15, 16 (Terry Whittaker); Getty Images pp. 8 (Johnny Johnson), 27 (Michael S. Quinton), 28 (Joseph Van Os), 29 (Doug Allan); naturepl.com pp. 11, 12 (© Warwick Sloss), 19, 20 (© Tom Mangelsen), 21, 22 (© Ian McCarthy); Photolibrary p. 9 (Owen Newman); Shutterstock pp. 4 (© Map Resources), 5 (© YellowSummer), 13, 14 (© Mark Yarchoan), 17, 18 (© Vladimir Melnik), 23, 24 (© Morten Hilmer); Visuals Unlimited, Inc. pp. 10 (© Rick Poley), 25, 26 (© Joe McDonald).

Cover image of an Arctic fox used with permission of Getty Images (Paul Nicklen).

We would like to thank Michael Bright for his invaluable help in the preparation of this book.

Every effort has been made to contact copyright holders of any material reproduced in this book. Any omissions will be rectified in subsequent printings if notice is given to the publisher.

All the Internet addresses (URLs) given in this book were valid at the time of going to press. However, due to the dynamic nature of the Internet, some addresses may have changed, or sites may have changed or ceased to exist since publication. While the author and publisher regret any inconvenience this may cause readers, no responsibility for any such changes can be accepted by either the author or the publisher.

# Contents

Some words are printed in bold, **like this**. You can find out what they mean by looking in the glossary.

# What Are Polar Regions Like?

Polar regions are cold, icy places. Earth's polar regions are the Arctic and the Antarctic. The Sun's rays are not strong in polar regions. This means the weather is cold.

The places at the top and bottom of this map are the coldest.

Pieces of ice float in Arctic seas.

Parts of polar regions are icy or snowy all the time. The edges of polar regions have warmer temperatures. There, the snow and ice melt in summer.

# Living in Polar Regions

Many animals could not live in polar regions. Polar animals must live in very cold weather. How do they **survive**?

Parts of polar regions stay dark for months at a time!

A thick layer of fat helps keep a walrus warm in the Arctic.

Polar animals have special **features** that help them **survive** in the cold. These features are called **adaptations**.

# What Is Camouflage?

**Camouflage** (KAM-uh-flaj) is an **adaptation** that helps animals hide. The color of an animal's skin, fur, or feathers may match the things around it.

Reindeer have brown coats that help them **blend in** with the things around them.

Camouflage helps keep young animals like these fox cubs safe.

Many polar animals change color. They turn white in winter to hide in the snow. In the summer, they grow dark fur or feathers. This helps them hide in rocks and soil.

**Predators** are animals that eat other animals. **Prey** animals are animals that predators eat. **Camouflage** helps both kinds of animals hide.

Eggs can be camouflaged, too. These eggs look like pebbles.

# Find the Polar Animals

CAMOUFLAGED

## Polar bear

Polar bears live only in the Arctic. Their white fur **blends in** with snow and ice. It helps hide them when they hunt for food.

Polar bears are very good swimmers. They have a thick layer of fat called blubber. The blubber keeps the bears warm in the icy water.

# Ptarmigan

A ptarmigan (TAR-mi-guhn) is a type of bird. Ptarmigans have dark feathers in summer. Females make nests on the ground. Their color helps keep them safe from foxes and owls.

CAMOUFLAGED

In winter, snow covers the ground. The
ptarmigans lose their dark feathers.
They grow white feathers. This lets them
**blend in** with the snow.

## Arctic hare

Arctic hares change color, too. Their fur is snowy white in winter. They grow gray or brown fur in summer. Their fur color helps them hide from **predators**, such as wolves and foxes.

CAMOUFLAGED

Arctic hares have another **adaptation** that lets them **survive** in the cold. Animals lose heat through their ears. So Arctic hares have short ears. This helps them stay warm.

REVEALED

## Harp seal

Some **predators** hunt young **prey** animals because they are weak. Young harp seals have fluffy, white fur. This helps the young seals **blend in** with the ice.

As harp seals grow, their fur turns gray and black. Adult seals spend most of their lives in the water. Their gray fur is better **camouflage** in the water than white fur would be.

## Ermine

Ermine (ER-muhn) are a kind of weasel. Their fur is dark on the top parts of their bodies. The underneath parts are white. The tips of their tails are black.

Ermine that live in very cold places turn white in the winter. Can you guess why? But the tips of their tails stay black all year round!

REVEALED

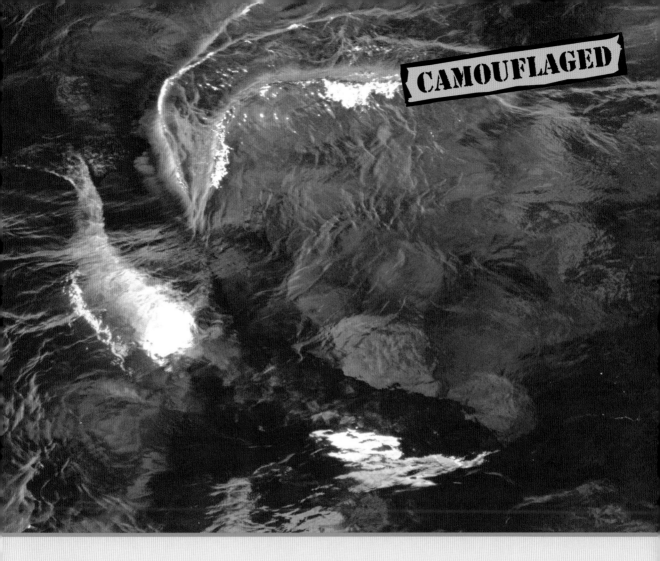

# Orca

Orcas (OR-kuhz) are also known as killer whales. It seems like their black and white color should make them easy to see. But it actually helps them hide in the water!

An animal looking down in the water may not spot an orca. Its black back can **blend in** with the ocean floor. An animal looking up might think the orca's white belly looks like sunlight on the ocean.

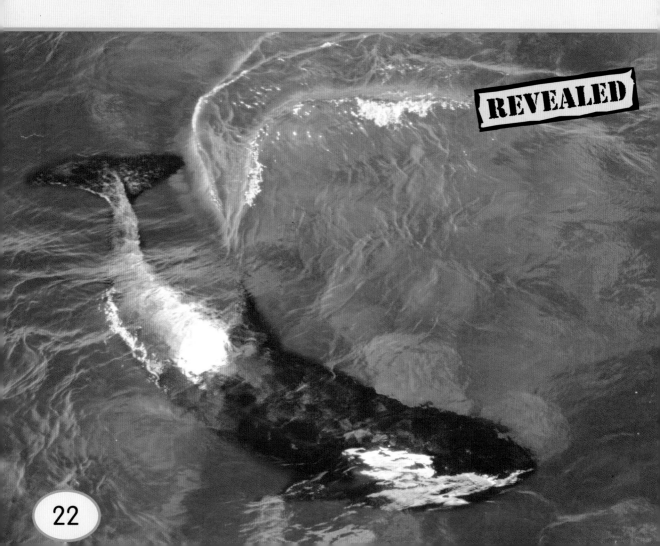

REVEALED

# Arctic fox

Arctic foxes have brown or gray coats in summer. They can hide in soil. In winter, their coats turn snowy white. The foxes can hide in snow. Blending in helps them sneak up on other animals as they hunt.

CAMOUFLAGED

Arctic foxes hunt for small animals, birds, and fish. Sometimes a fox will follow a polar bear. It hopes to eat the bear's leftovers! The fox's coat helps it hide so the bear doesn't eat it.

**CAMOUFLAGED**

## Snowy owl

Snowy owls live in the Arctic. Sometimes they travel south to find food. The owls' **camouflage** helps them hide from foxes and wolves. It also helps them hide as they wait for **prey**.

Snowy owls eat small animals, such as mice and lemmings. The owls are very good at hearing. They can hear other animals moving beneath the snow!

REVEALED

These Dall sheep would be camouflaged in the snow—if it weren't for their big horns!

**Camouflage** helps polar animals hide. It helps some animals hunt. It helps other animals hide from **predators**. Camouflage helps polar animals **survive** in their cold surroundings.

# Animals that Stand Out

Emperor penguins do not need to hide when they are on land. No land animals hunt them. Penguins only hunt in the sea.

Emperor penguins are easy to spot when they stand on the Antarctic ice.

The penguins' dark backs and light bellies help them hide in the water.

When the penguins swim, their colors help hide them. Like orcas, their black backs and white bellies make them hard to see underwater.

# Glossary

**adaptation** feature that helps an animal survive in its surroundings

**blend in** matches well with the things around it

**camouflage** adaptation that helps an animal blend in

**feature** special part of an animal

**predator** animal that eats other animals

**prey** animal that other animals eat

**survive** stay alive

# Find Out More

## Books to read

*Arctic and Antarctic.* New York: DK Publishing, 2006.

Helman, Andrea. *Caribou Crossing: Animals of the Arctic National Wildlife Refuge.* Seattle: Sasquatch Books, 2009.

## Websites

**www.aad.gov.au/default.asp?casid=1134**
Antarctic information from the Australian Antarctic Division.

**www.antarctica.ac.uk/about_antarctica/wildlife/index.php**
Antarctic wildlife information from the British Antarctic Survey.

**www.kids.nationalgeographic.com/Photos/Arctic-animals**
Photos of Arctic animals from National Geographic.

# Index